# Hooked On Easy Piano Classics

## CONTENTS

© 1982 **JOE GOLDFEDER MUSIC ENTERPRISES & MUSIC BOX DANCER PUBLICATIONS LTD.**

# CANON IN D

Johann Pachelbel
Arr. Edwin McLean

COPYRIGHT© 1982 **Music Box Dancer Publications Ltd.**,
International Copyright secured. Printed in Canada. All Rights Reserved.

Canon In D 2/2 E.P.

# CAPRICE

PAGANINI

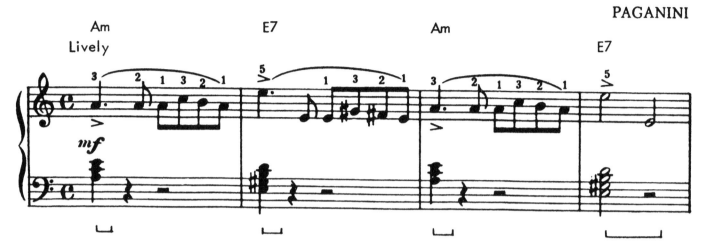

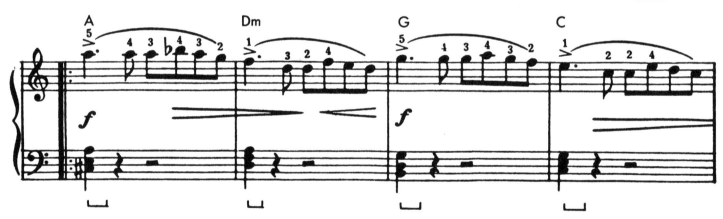

# CONCERTO IN A MINOR

E. GRIEG

# CHOPSTICKS

DE LULLI

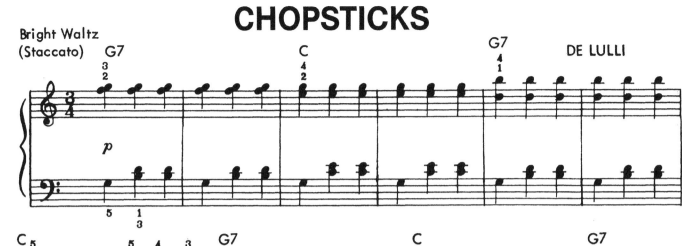

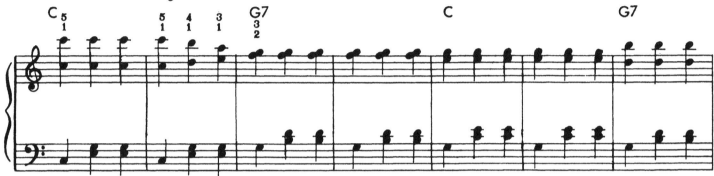

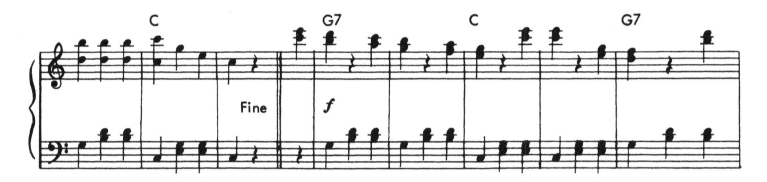

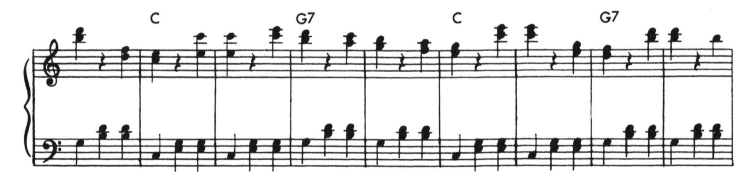

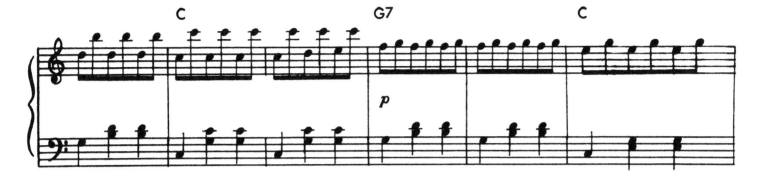

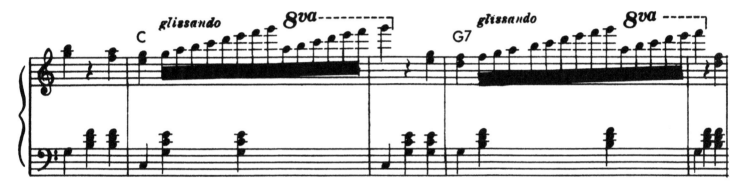

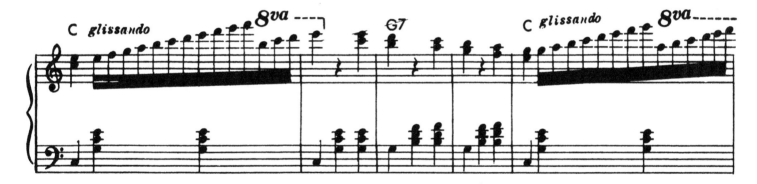

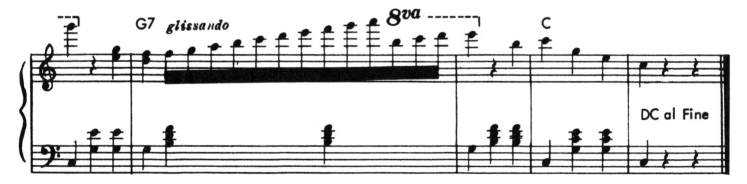

CHOPSTICKS  2 of 2

# CONCERTO NO. 1

P. TSCHAIKOWSKY

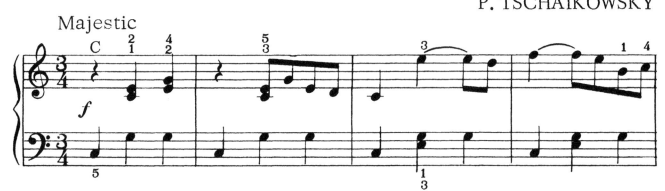

# THE ENTERTAINER
*A Rag Time Two Step*

Scott Joplin
Arr: Edwin McLean

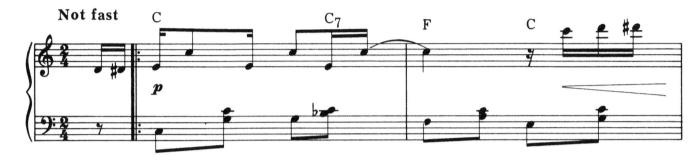

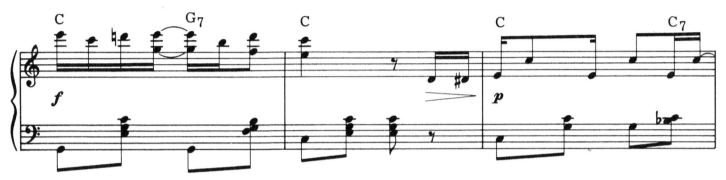

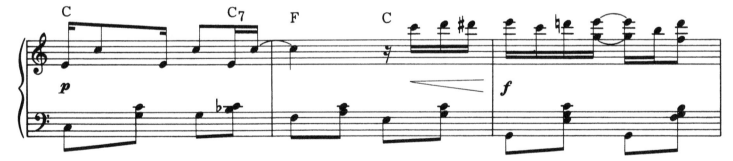

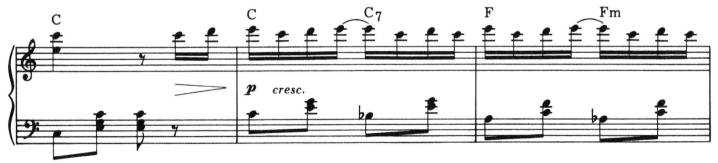

©Copyright 1980 MUSIC BOX DANCER PUBLICATIONS LTD.

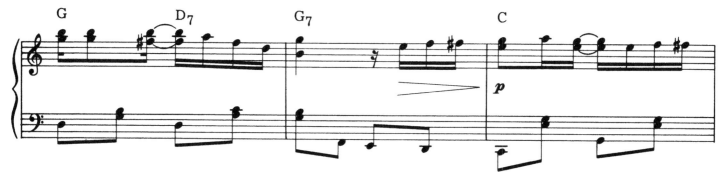

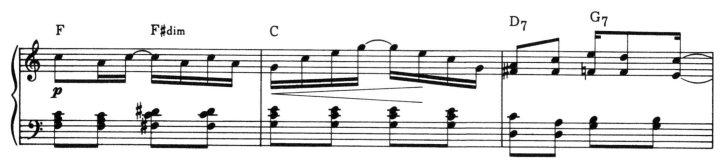

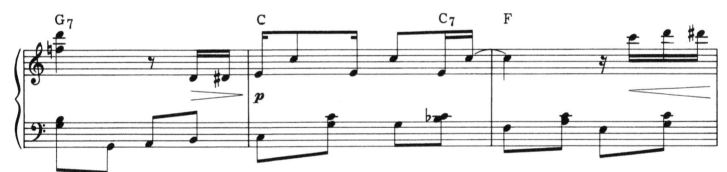

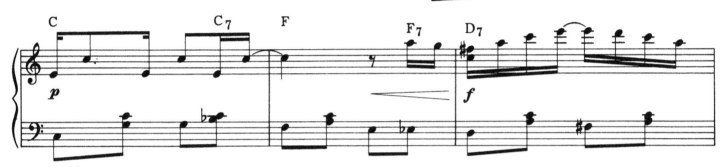

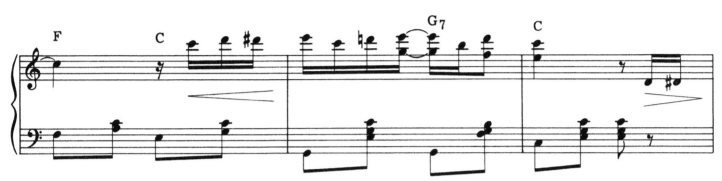

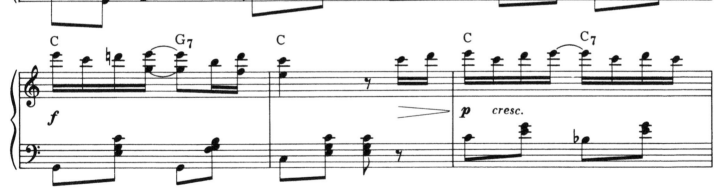

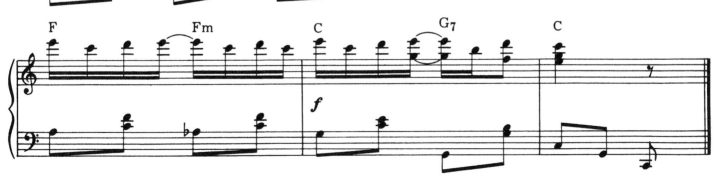

# FÜR ELISE

L. van BEETHOVEN

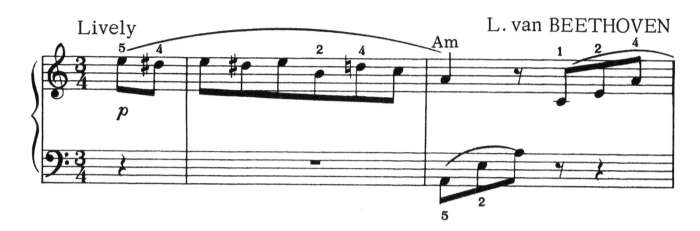

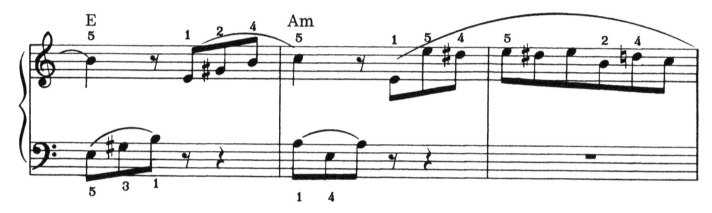

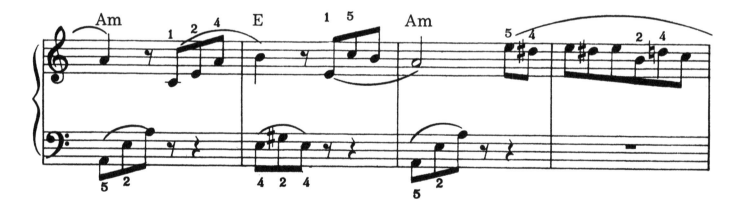

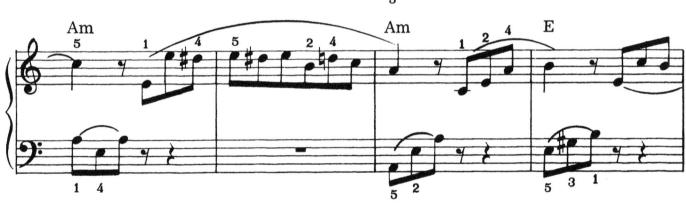

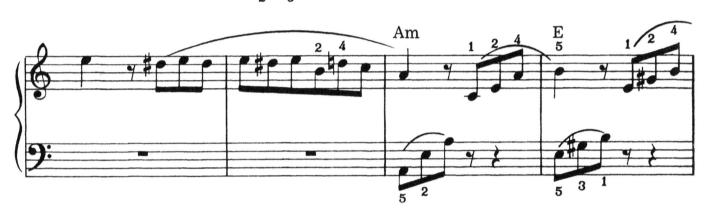

# JESU, JOY OF MAN'S DESIRING

Arr: Edwin McLean

J.S.Bach
From Cantata Nº. 147

# LARGO

### (FROM "NEW WORLD SYMPHONY")

DVOŘÁK

Largo

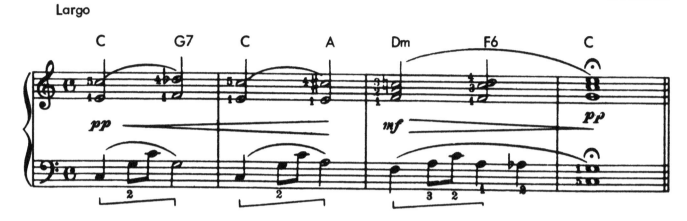

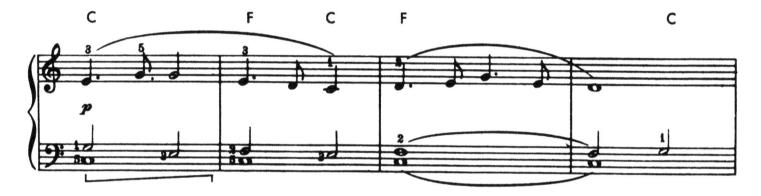

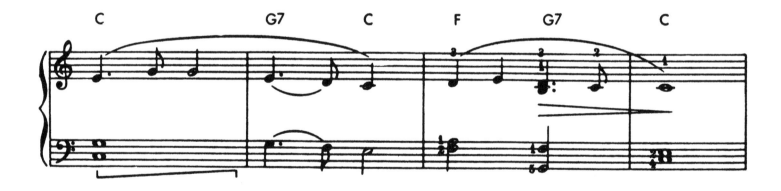

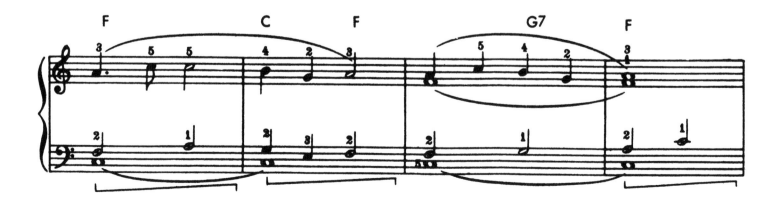

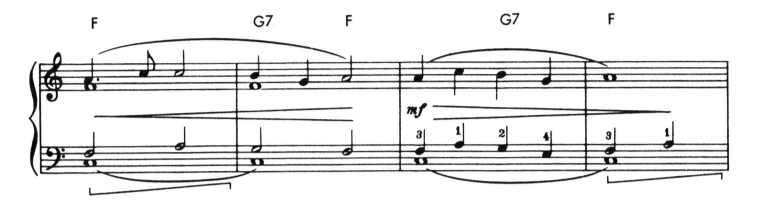

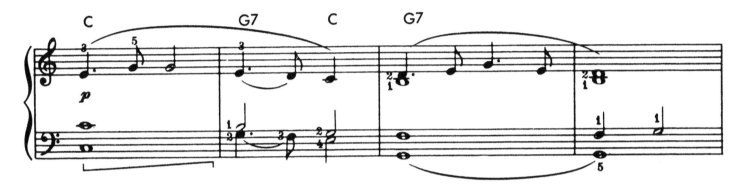

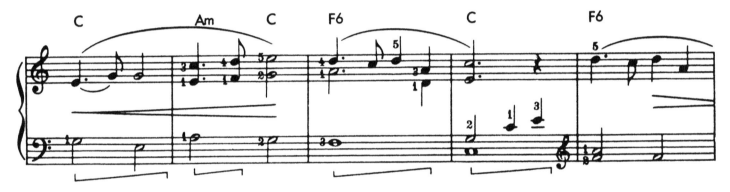

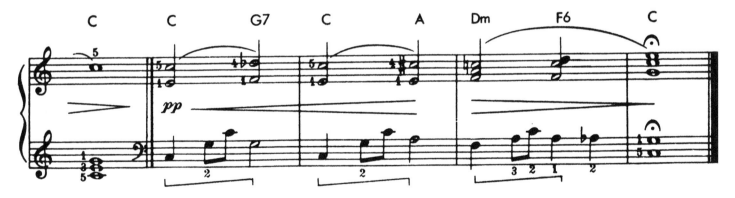

LARGO  2 of 2

# LARGO

Broadly

G. F. HANDEL

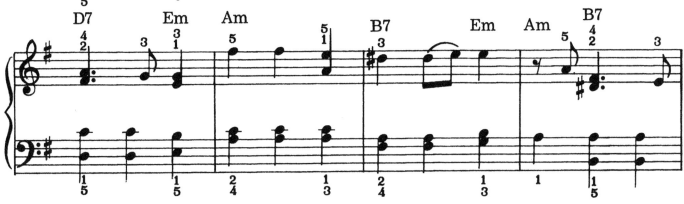

# LIEBESTRAUM

Rather lively

F. LISZT

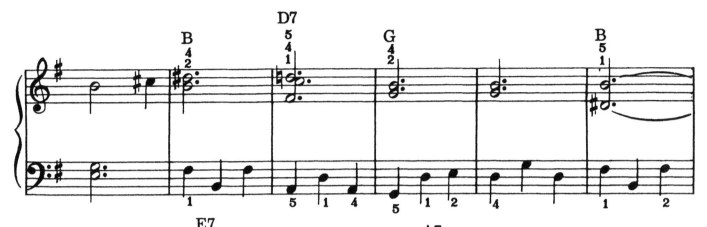

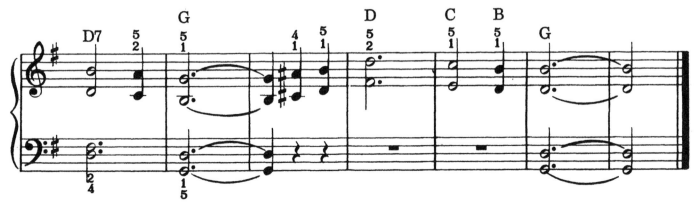

# LULLABY
## (CRADLE SONG)

BRAHMS

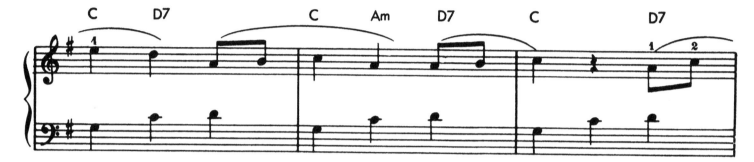

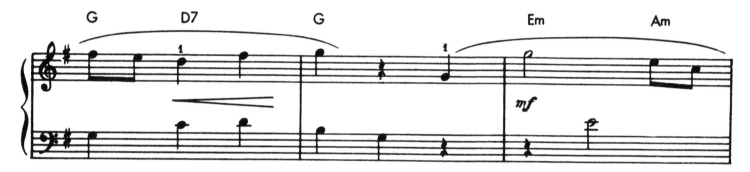

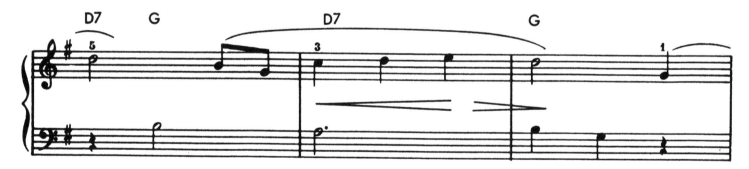

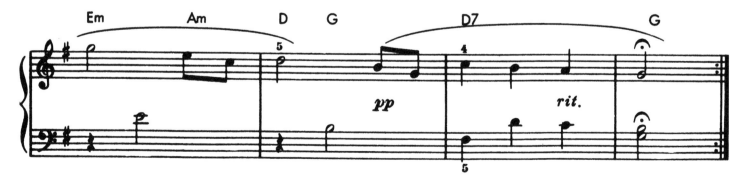

# MARCH MILITAIRE

SCHUBERT
Opus 51 — No. 1

# MELODY IN F

RUBINSTEIN

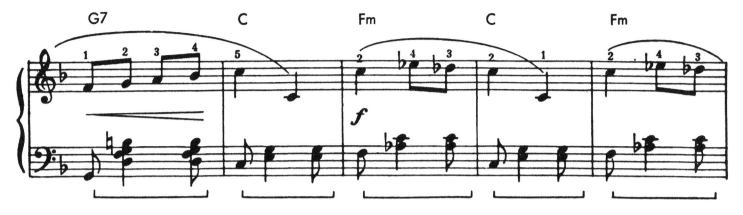

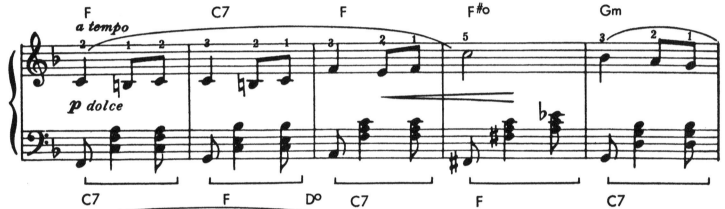

MELODY IN F   2 of 2

# MILITARY POLONAISE

## Op. 40 No. I

F. CHOPIN

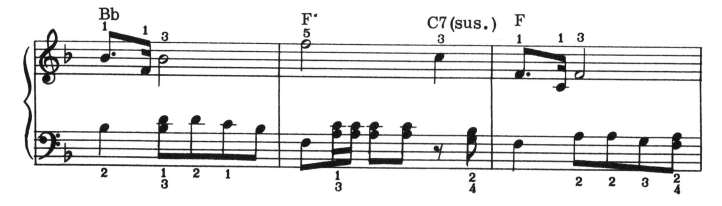

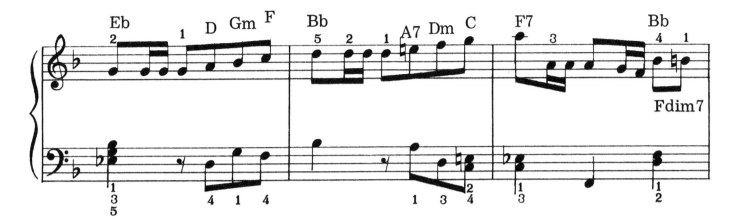

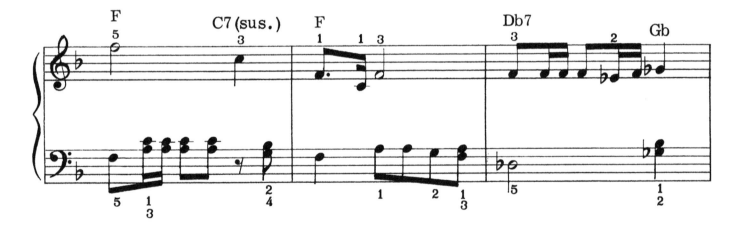

*D. C. al Fine*

# MINUET IN G

Menuet style

L. van BEETHOVEN

*very smoothly*

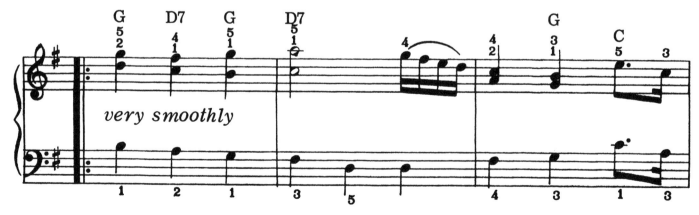

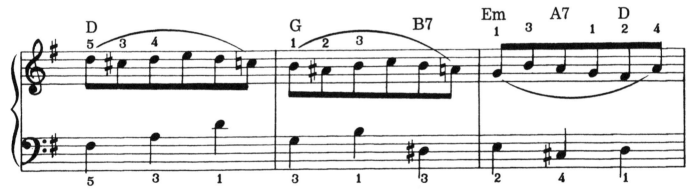

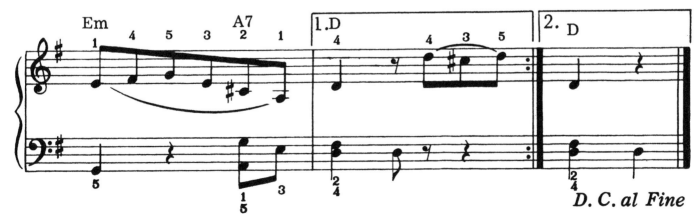

# MOONLIGHT SONATA

Slowly

L. van BEETHOVEN

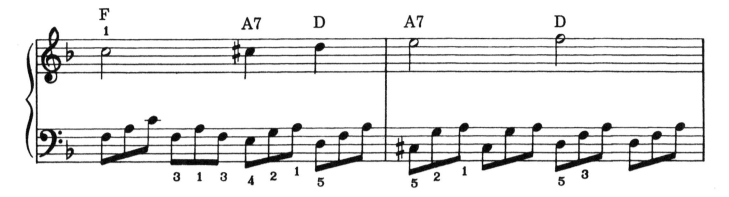
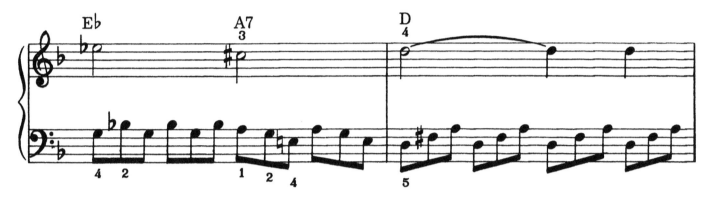

# MUSETTE

## from the Note Book of Anna Magdalene Bach

JOHANN SEBASTIAN BACH

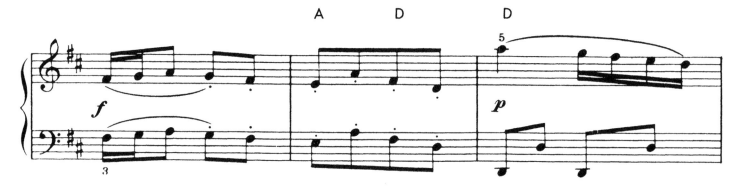

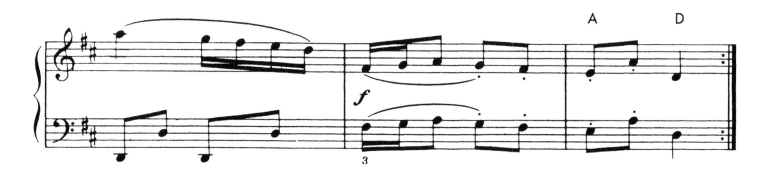

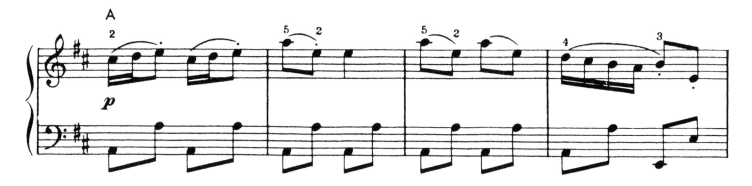

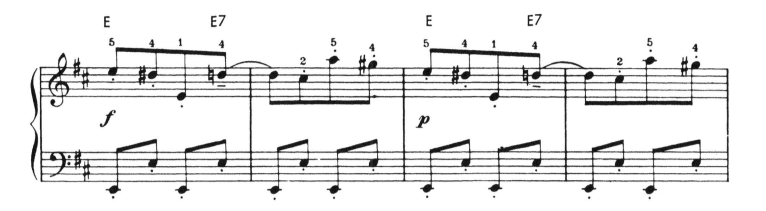

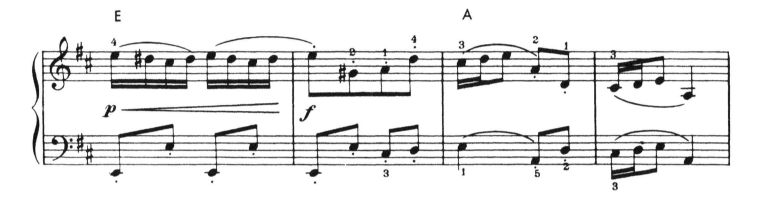

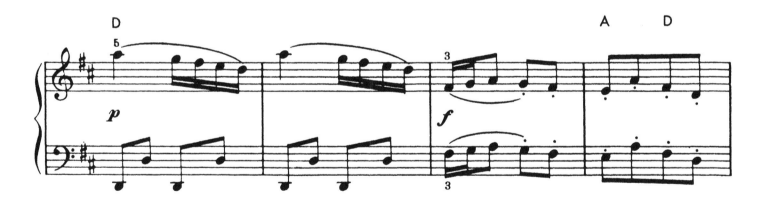

# ODE TO JOY

## *Theme from Symphony No.9 in D Major*

Ludwig van Beethoven
Arr: Edwin McLean

COPYRIGHT © 1982 **Music Box Dancer Publications Ltd.**,
International Copyright secured. Printed in Canada. All Rights Reserved.

# PIZZICATO POLKA

DELIBES

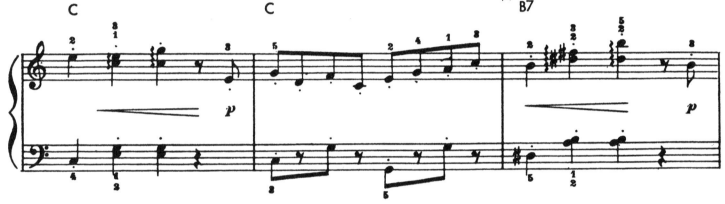

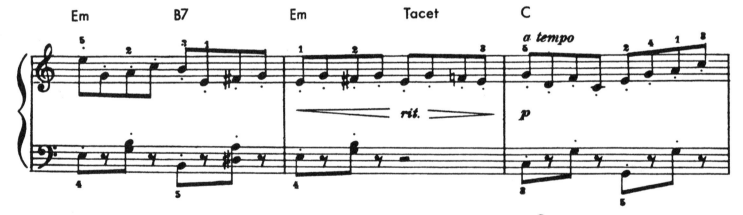

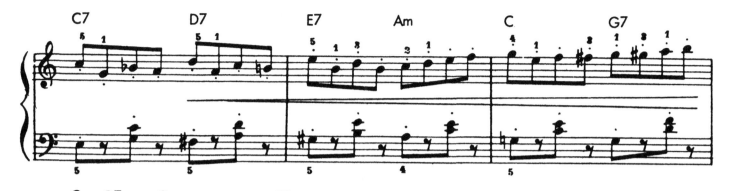

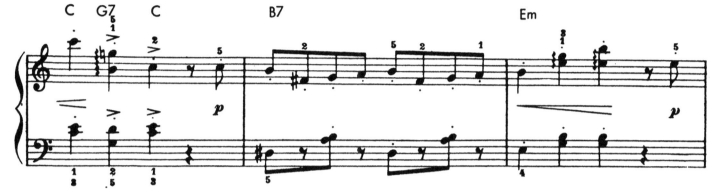

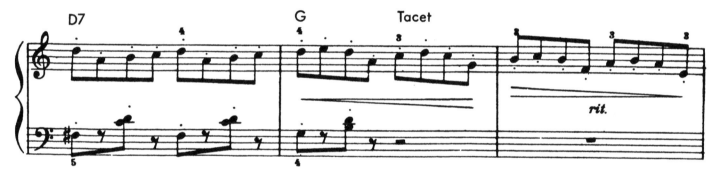

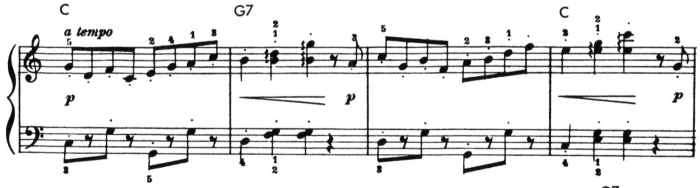

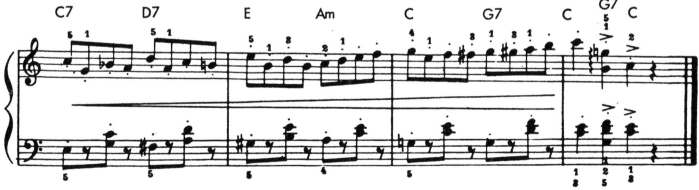

# PLAISIR D'AMOUR

G. P. Martini
Arr. Edwin McLean

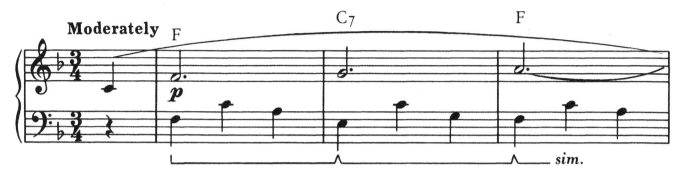

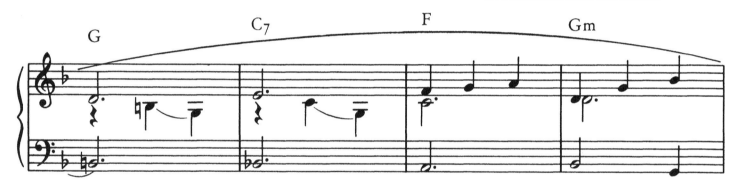

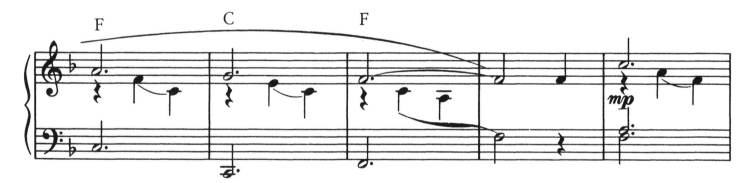

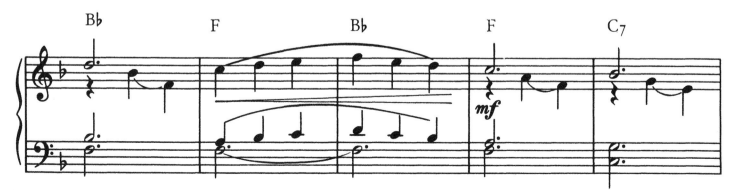

COPYRIGHT © 1982 Music Box Dancer Publications Ltd.,
International Copyright secured. Printed in Canada. All Rights Reserved.
Unauthorized copying, arranging, adapting, recording or public performance is an infringement of copyright.
Infringers are liable under the law.

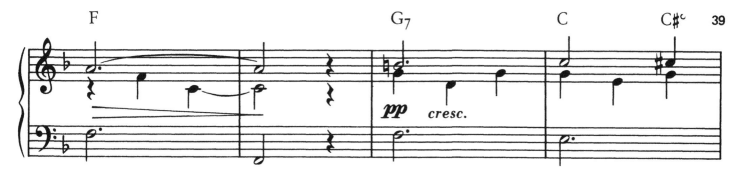

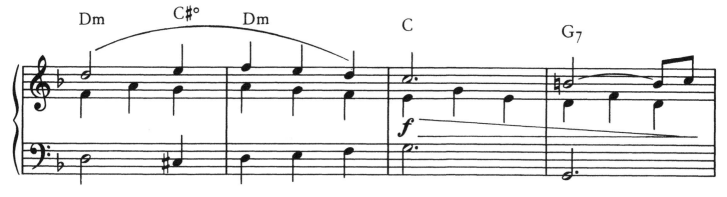

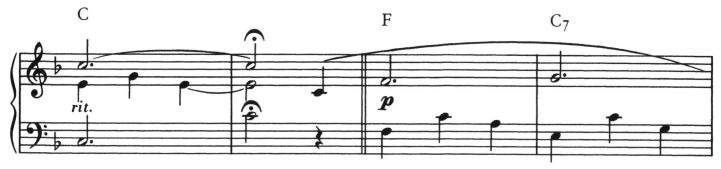

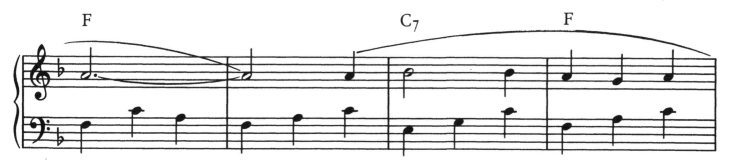

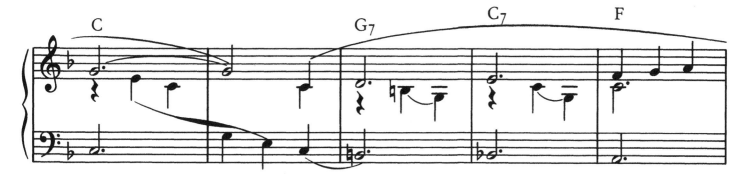

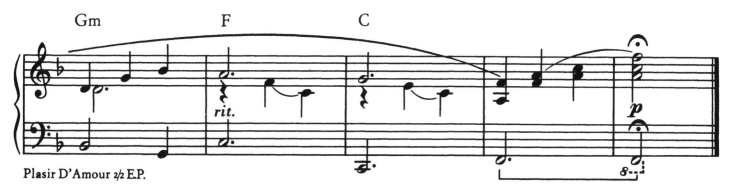

Plasir D'Amour 2/2 E.P.

# POLOVETZIAN DANCE

# PRELUDE

## (OPUS 28, NO. 6)

CHOPIN

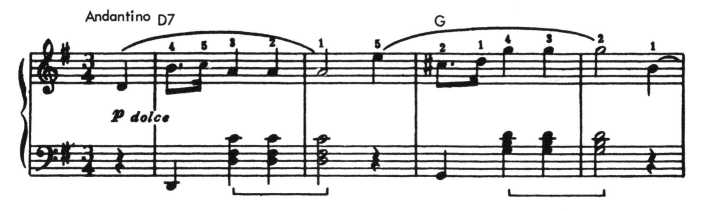

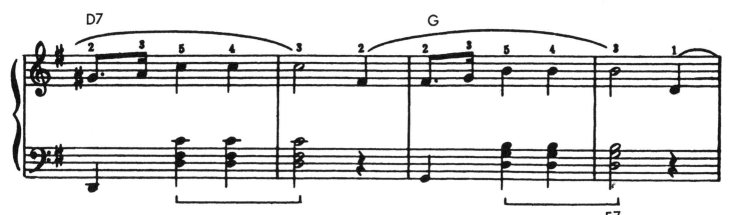

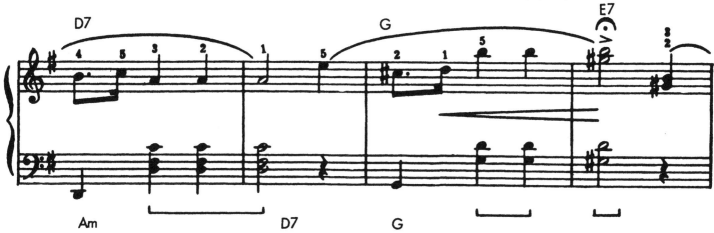

PRELUDE 1 of 1

# POLKA FROM "ORPHEUS"

OFFENBACH

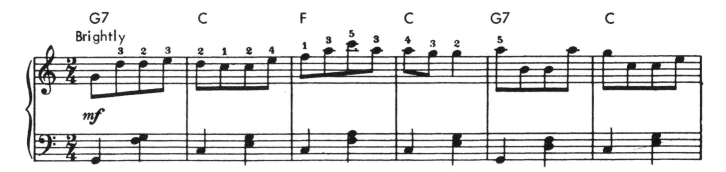

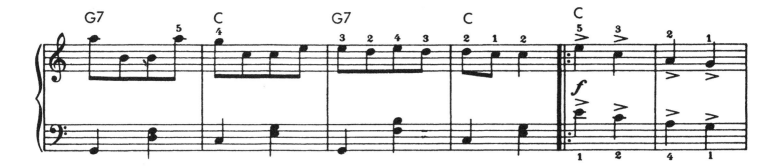

# ROMEO AND JULIET

P. TSCHAIKOWSKY

Moderately slow (with expression)

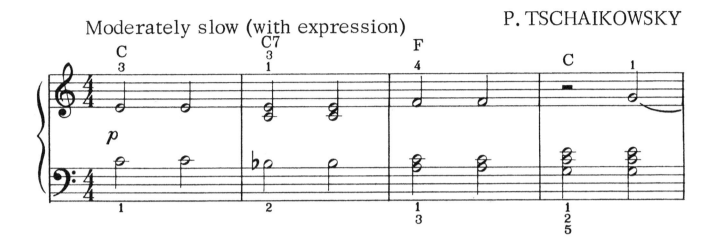

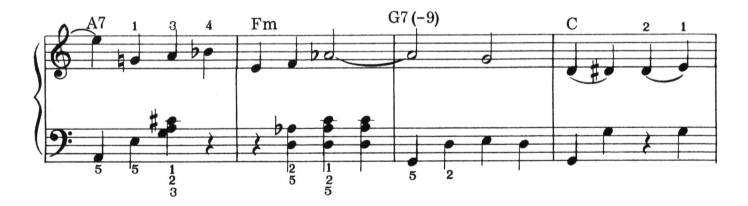

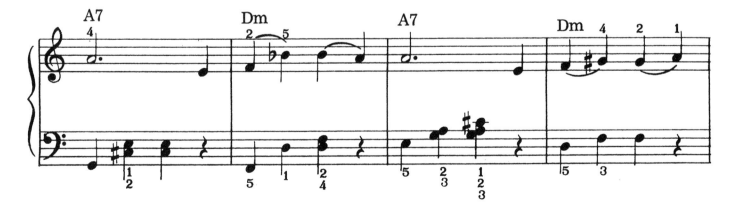

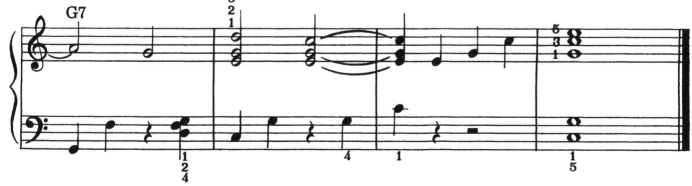

# THE SKATERS WALTZ

Arr. Edwin McLean

Emil Waldteufel
*Op. 183*

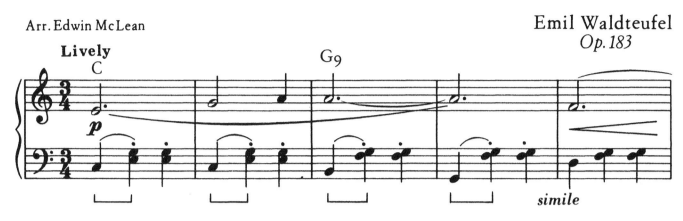

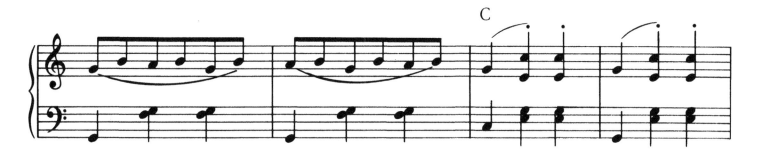

The Skaters Waltz 2/2

# SONATA IN C MAJOR

Brightly

W. A. MOZART

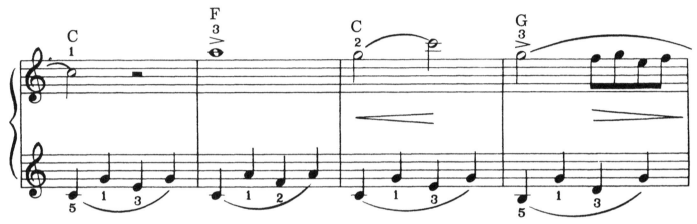

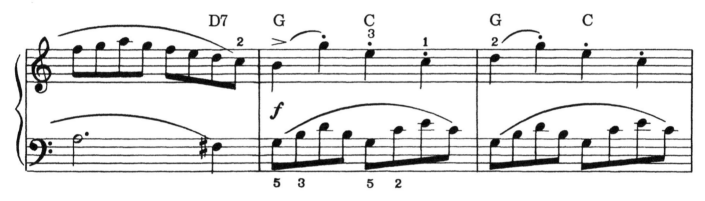

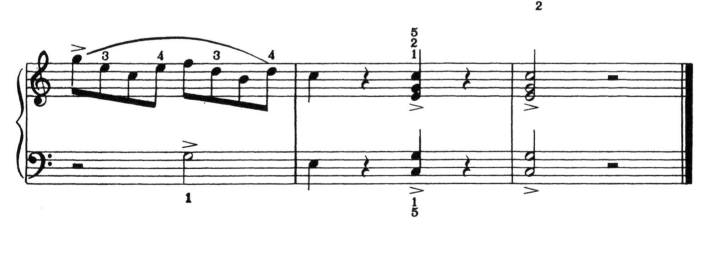

# SURPRISE SYMPHONY

### (THEME)

HAYDN

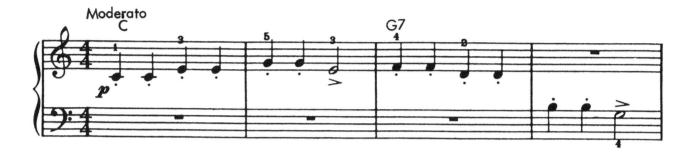

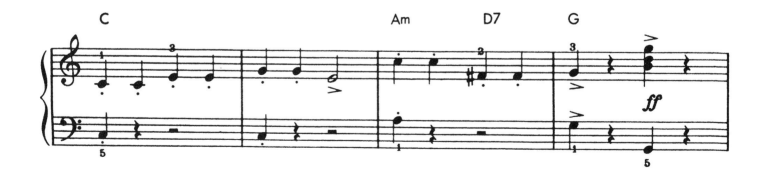

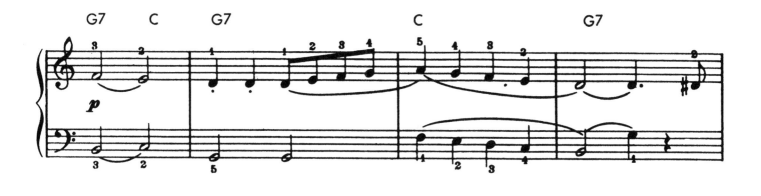

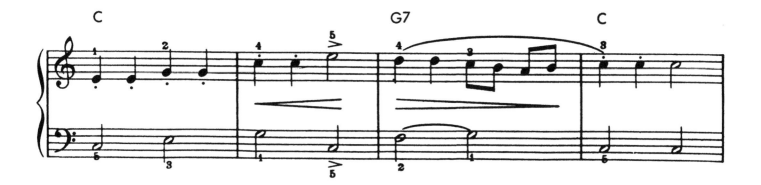

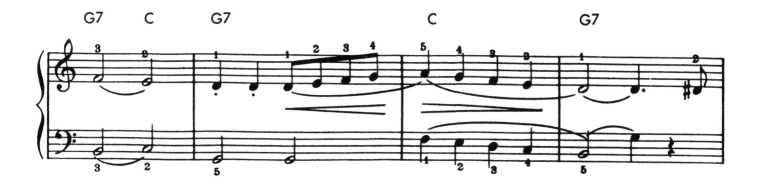

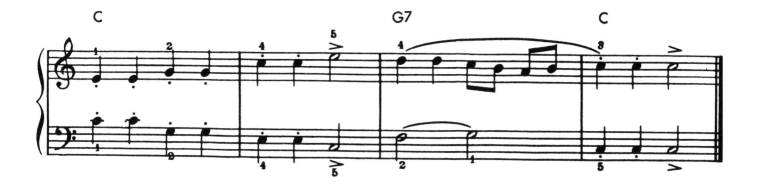

# SONATA IN A

## (THEME)

MOZART

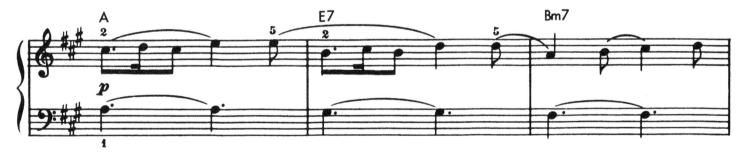

# SYMPHONY PATHETIQUE

Slowly with expression

P.TSCHAIKOWSKY

# TO A WILD ROSE

EDWARD MacDOWELL

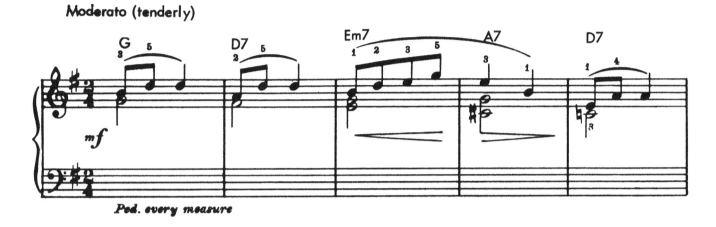

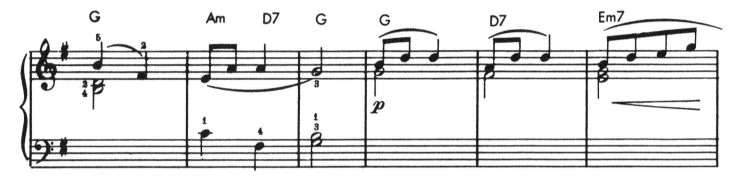

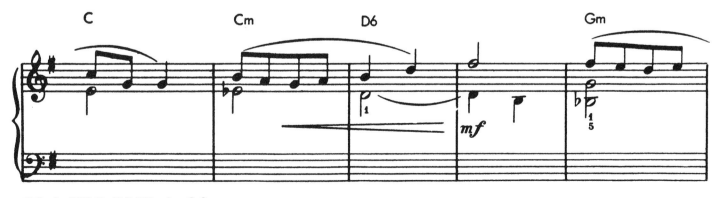

TO A WILD ROSE  1 of 2

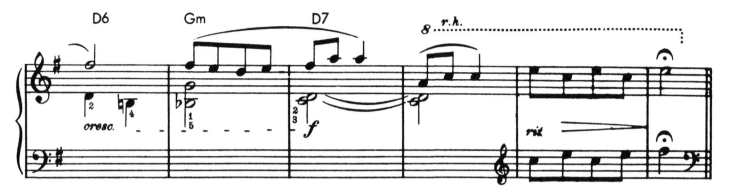

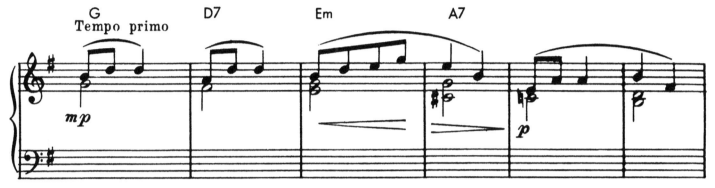

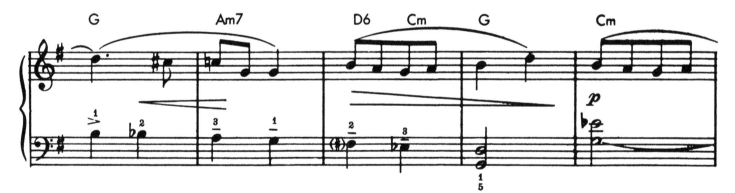

\* **This G may be omitted**

TO A WILD ROSE 2 of 2

# TOREADOR SONG
### (FROM "CARMEN")

BIZET

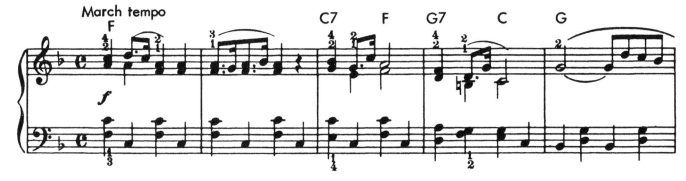

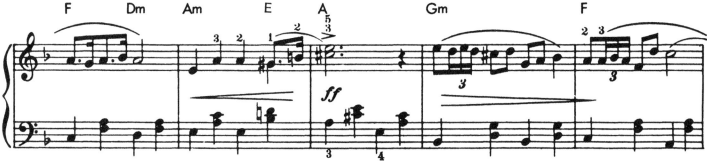

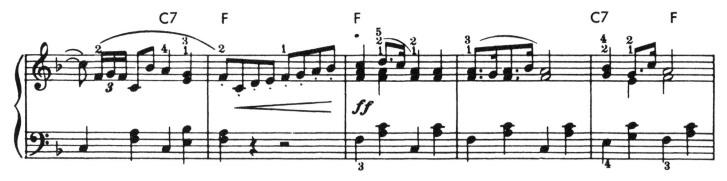

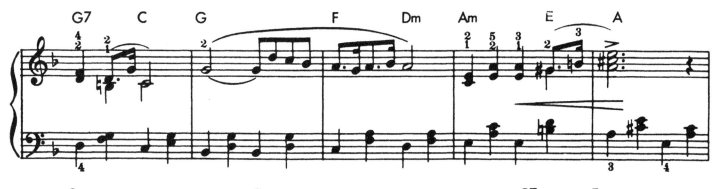

# BLUE DANUBE WALTZ

JOHANN STRAUSS

BLUE DANUBE WALTZ  1 of 3

58

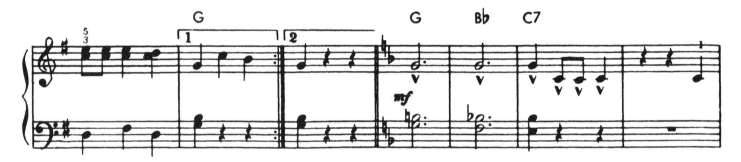

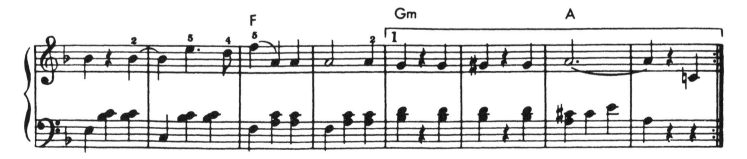

BLUE DANUBE WALTZ  2 of 3

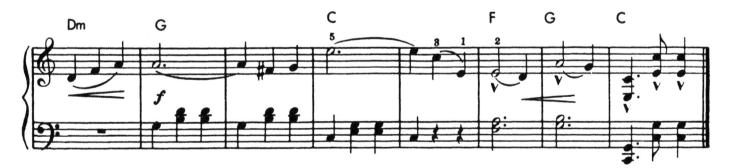

# WALTZ OF THE FLOWERS
## (FROM "NUTCRACKER SUITE")

TSCHAIKOWSKY

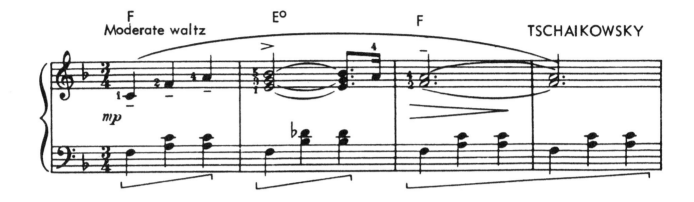

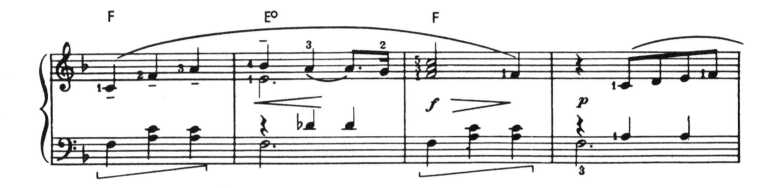

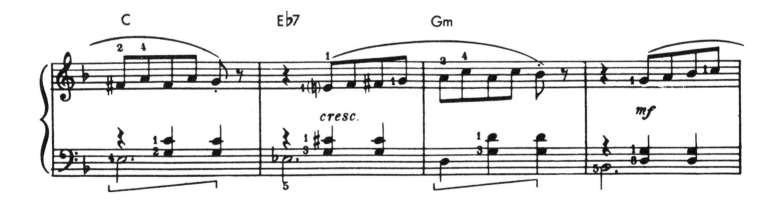

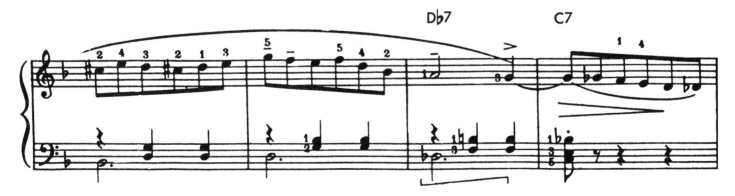

WALTZ OF THE FLOWERS 1 of 2

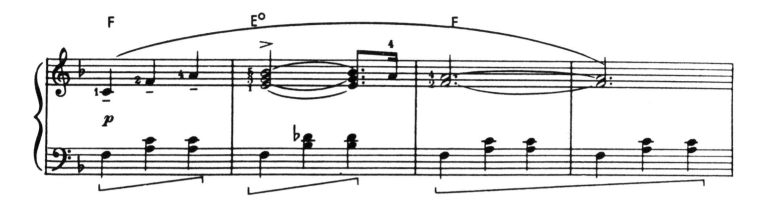

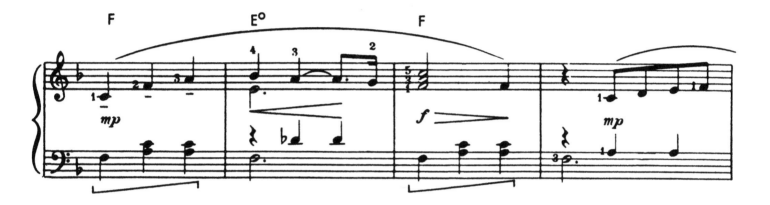

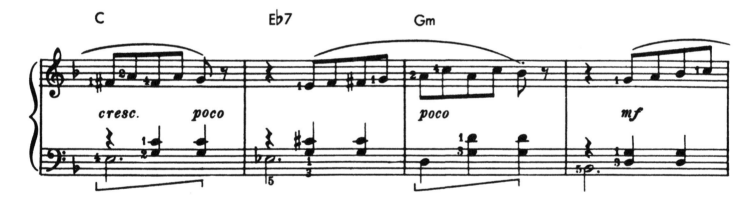

WALTZ OF THE FLOWERS 2 of 2

# WILLIAM TELL

G. ROSSINI

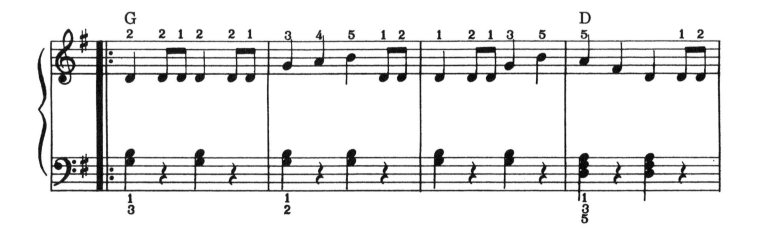

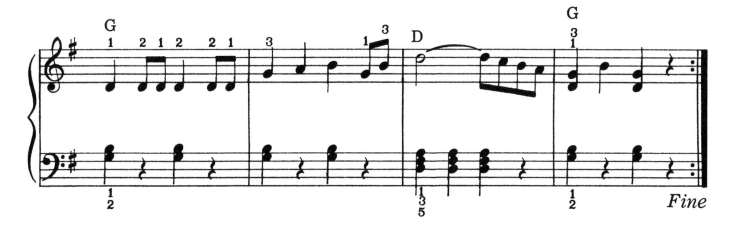

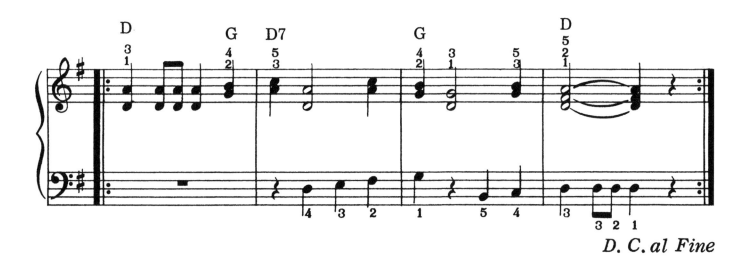

# A World of Unforgettable Music at Your Finger Tips

MORE

## EASY PIANO ARRANGEMENTS by ARTHUR BAYAS

### VOLUME ONE

*Contents*

AMARYLLIS *(GHYS)*
CLAIR DE LUNE *(Debussy)*
CONCERTO IN A MINOR *(Grieg)*
CONCERTO #1 *(Tschaikowsky)*
FANTASIE IMPROMPTU *(Chopin)*
FINLANDIA *(Sibelius)*
FÜR ELISE *(Beethoven)*
GLOW WORM *(Lincke)*
HUNGARIAN RHAPSODY #2 *(Liszt)*
LARGO *(Dvořák)*
LARGO *(Handel)*
LIEBESTRAUM *(Liszt)*
LULLABY *(Brahms)*
MEDITATION *(Massenet)*
MELODY IN F *(Rubinstein)*
MELODY OF LOVE *(Engelmann)*
MILITARY POLONAISE *(Chopin)*
MINUET *(Paderewski)*
MINUET IN G *(Beethoven)*
MINUTE WALTZ *(Chopin)*
MOONIGHT SONATA *(Beethoven)*
NOCTURNE *(Chopin)*
OLD REFRAIN, THE
POLONAISE OP. 53 *(Chopin)*
POLOVETZIAN DANCE *(Borodin)*
PRELUDE *(Rachmaninoff)*
REVERIE *(Debussy)*
REVERIE *(Schumann)*
ROMEO AND JULIET *(Tschaikowsky)*
SABRE DANCE *(Khachaturian)*
SONATA IN C MAJOR *(Mozart)*
SYMPHONY PATHETIQUE *(Tschaikowsky)*
TO A WILD ROSE *(MacDowell)*
UNFINISHED SYMPHONY *(Schubert)*
WILLIAM TELL *(Rossini)*

### VOLUME TWO

*Contents*

AIR *(Mozart)*
BAGATELLE *(Diabelli)*
BLUE DANUBE WALTZ *(Strauss)*
BRIDAL CHORUS *(Wagner)*
CAPRICE *(Paganini)*
CHOPSTICKS *(De Lulli)*
DANCING DOLL *(Poldini)*
ENTERTAINER, THE *(Joplin)*
EVENING STAR *(Wagner)*
FAREWELL TO THE PIANO *(Beethoven)*
HEDGE ROSES *(Schubert)*
HUNGARIAN DANCE #6 *(Brahms)*
HUNGARIAN TUNE *(Bartok)*
IN A LITTLE FRENCH VILLAGE
  *(Tschaikowsky)*
LITTLE MINUET *(Beethoven)*
LITTLE SCHERZO *(Kabalevsky)*
MARCH MILITAIRE *(Schubert)*
MERRY WIDOW WALTZ *(Lehar)*
MUSSETTE *(Bach)*
PARADE OF THE TIN SOLDIERS *(Jessel)*
PIZZICATO POLKA *(Delibes)*
POEM, THE *(Fibich)*
POLKA *(Offenbach)*
PRELUDE *(Opus 28, #6) (Chopin)*
PRELUDE IN C♯ MINOR *(Rachmaninoff)*
ROSAMUNDE *(Schubert)*
SIMPLE THEME *(Mozart)*
SKATERS' WALTZ *(Waldteufel)*
SOLDIERS' MARCH *(Schumann)*
SONATA IN A *(Mozart)*
SURPRISE SYMPHONY *(Haydn)*
TOREADOR SONG *(Bizet)*
TURKISH MARCH *(Beethoven)*
WALTZ *(Brahms)*
WALTZ OF THE FLOWERS *(Tschaikowsky)*
WILD HORSEMAN, THE *(Schumann)*

*We shall be very happy to answer all inquiries.*
*Please write for catalogs to:*

## JOE GOLDFEDER MUSIC ENTERPRISES
P.O. **Box 660**, Lynbrook, N. Y. 11563